Troublesome Children

A Guide to Understanding and
Managing Youth with
Attention Deficit Hyperactivity Disorder
Oppositional Defiant Disorder and
Conduct Disorder

by

Jalal Shamsie
M.B., F.R.C.P.(C), F.R.C.Psych.

Professor of Psychiatry, University of Toronto
Director, Institute for the study of Antisocial behaviour in Youth

A publication of the
Institute for the study of Antisocial behaviour in Youth
250 College Street, Toronto, Ontario, M5T 1R8

Institute for the study of
Antisocial behaviour in Youth
250 College Street
Toronto, Ontario M5T 1R8

Printed in Canada

ISBN 0-9680015-0-5

Dedicated to those who choose
to work with troublesome children

Acknowledgements

I am indebted to the many parents who came to see me with their children, who talked to me about their children's behaviour and their frustrations. Through working with them I learned much that I share in this book. I owe a special gratitude to two colleagues of mine, without whose help this book would have never materialized, Cynthia Sykes and Hayley Hamilton. I am also grateful to Dr. Susan Bradley, Dr. Thaddeus Ulzen and Charlie Knight who reviewed the manuscript and made many helpful suggestions.

Table of Contents

Preface

This book provides clinically relevant information on three disorders: attention deficit hyperactivity disorder, oppositional defiant disorder, and conduct disorder Most of the troublesome children suffer from one or more of these disorders. These children, who are more troublesome than troubled, form the largest group of children who are referred to children's mental health centres and professionals. The reason to present information on all three disorders is twofold. First, there is a great deal of comorbidity; the same child may have more than one disorder. The second reason is that some children develop one disorder after another, thus experiencing all the three disorders as they grow from early childhood to adolescence. This book provides information on the three disorders in the same format, so that the reader can understand the similarities and differences.

There is no attempt made to present all the information available, only the information which is relevant to persons living or working with these children. This book is aimed at mental health professionals, students in mental health disciplines, parents and teachers. It is written in point form whenever possible so that information is succinctly stated and can be easily located. Technical terms are seldom used, and when used, are explained. Recognizing that most workers in the field have limited time to study, the book is kept to a minimal size. Relevant references are provided so that more detailed information can be located.

As is evident by reading this book, troublesome children are themselves victims. They have been unfortunate to inherit disorders and disabilities. They have been unable to receive the care and controls which are so necessary for children to grow emotionally. Though they cause trouble to others, in the long run, they only hurt themselves. It is in the interest of the society to help them when they are young so that they are less likely to commit criminal acts when they become adults.

This book is dedicated to those who choose to work with troublesome children, a commitment that requires immense patience and a capacity to respond therapeutically despite provocation.

Introduction

Children, like other living beings, are shaped by genes and the environment. Genes provide the characteristics that the offspring gets from the two parents. These include not only colour, height and intelligence, but also temperament. Environment includes not only everything that happens to the baby after it is born, but also the environment the fetus experiences during the nine months of its gestation. It is suggested that most of the behaviour of an adult human is determined by its genetic inheritance and early experiences during childhood. Therefore, to understand why some children become antisocial and violent it is important to examine both the genetic and environmental characteristics which may make the child violent.

Genetic factors which may promote the development of antisocial behaviour include disorders such as attention deficit hyperactivity disorder, reading and other learning disabilities and difficult temperament. A child born with a difficult temperament has such characteristics as persistent crying and difficulties sleeping and feeding. Environmental characteristics which may promote antisocial behaviour include a lack of care and a lack of controls. For children to grow emotionally and socially they need at least one adult who is there for them, providing the nurturing and a caring relationship as well as teaching them socially acceptable behaviour. Violent behaviour is most likely to develop when a child born with special needs experiences a non-caring and non-understanding environment. It is the combination of negative genetic and environmental factors which promotes the development of antisocial behaviour [1,2].

Though genetic factors play a critical role in the development of a child, it has been shown that environmental factors can enhance or diminish the negative genetic effects. A child born with a difficult temperament, can grow up to be an adult, no different in any way from a child born with good temperament (3). However, to negate the effects of difficult temperament, the child needs an extraordinarily understanding environment. Therefore, a caring and understanding environment can overcome genetic factors, or at the very least, as in the case of attention deficit disorder, it can minimize the effects, and prevent the development of additional problems. To understand the behaviour of a child, it is important not only to assess the child, but to understand the environment. It is the response of the environment to the child's difficulties that determines the final outcome. It is the interaction between the child and the parent which should be the focus of study in understanding the antisocial behaviour and finding a suitable intervention.

Like children, all parents are not the same. Some are more patient, more understanding and have more energy than others. A child with difficult temperament may not be as troublesome to some parents as to others. Some children, whose parents are impatient, easily exasperated or depressed, may become more difficult as they experience less care. Therefore, it comes down to a match between a child and a parent. A good match results in a happy parent, and a satisfied child. A poor match can result in a parent getting increasingly exasperated and a child becoming increasingly difficult. Therefore, all problems related to children must be understood in the context of parent and child interaction.

Children with psychiatric disorders can be divided into two broad categories: children who are troubled by their disorder, and children whose disorders are more troublesome to others than to themselves. Some examples of troubled children are those who suffer from anxiety, depression, and phobias. Examples of troublesome children include children with attention deficit hyperactivity disorder (ADHD), oppositional defiant disorder (ODD), and conduct disorder (CD) (see Table 1). This book, as the title reports, is about troublesome children.

Table 1 - Children with Emotional Disorders

Troubled
    More disturbing to themselves than to others.
      e.g., depressive and anxiety disorders

Troublesome
    More disturbing to others than to themselves.
      e.g., attention deficit hyperactivity disorder, oppositional defiant disorder, conduct disorder

---

Troublesome children, need special attention for two important reasons. First, they form three fourths of all referrals to mental health clinics (4). Together they represent the largest group of children needing attention. Second, if untreated, their problems are likely to continue into adulthood, with serious consequences to themselves and society (5). Most of these children exhibit aggressive behaviour, which is the second most stable personality trait after intelligence (6). Aggressive behaviour once established, seems to continue, in adulthood even after many interventions to stop it. Most violent adults were aggressive and troublesome children (7). It has been shown that children grow up to be violent adolescents in a predictable and recognisable way (8). So, if society is concerned about violent youth, the easiest and the least expensive way to intervene is to identify and modify aggressive behaviour in children. The success rate is higher and it costs less. It is easier to treat an aggressive and destructive six year old child, than a sixteen year old.

1
Attention Deficit Hyperactivity Disorder(ADHD)

Characteristics

1. They are unable to concentrate and stay on track.
2. They are impulsive.
3. They are hyperactive.

The above symptoms are usually present before the child enters the school system. Most parents cope with the symptoms, believing that the child is just more active than others. These symptoms, however, come to the forefront in the classroom and often lead to referral to a professional. (See Table 2 for a complete description of symptoms and diagnostic criteria.)

Differential Diagnosis

The diagnosis of ADHD is not always easy as some children who do not suffer from the disorder, behave in a way that is very similar to ADHD children. These include children with anxiety and oppositional defiant disorder. Children who are anxious, usually because of some family disturbance, may be hyperactive but do not exhibit inattention and impulsivity. These children, if given the

Table 2 - Diagnostic Criteria For ADHD*

A. **Either (1) or (2):**

1. Six (or more) of the following symptoms of inattention for at least 6 months to a degree that is inconsistent with the developmental level:

    (a) often fails to give close attention to details or makes careless mistakes in school work, work or other activities

    (b) often has difficulty sustaining attention in tasks or play activities.

    (c) often does not listen when spoken to directly

    (d) often does not follow through on instructions and fails to finish school work, chores or duties in the workplace (not due to oppositional behaviour)

    (e) often has difficulty organizing tasks and activities

    (f) often avoids, dislikes, or is reluctant to engage in tasks that require sustained mental effort (such as school work)

    (g) often loses things necessary for tasks or activities (e.g., assignments, toys)

    (h) is often easily distracted by extraneous stimuli

    (i) is often forgetful in daily activities

* Based on DSM-IV (Diagnostic and Statistical Manual of Mental Disorders, 4th edition)

2. Six (or more) of the following symptoms of hyperactivity - impulsivity for at least six months:

Hyperactivity
(a) often fidgets with hands or feet or squirms in seat
(b) often leaves seat in classroom or in other situation in which remaining seated is expected
(c) often runs about or climbs excessively
(d) often has difficulty playing or engaging in leisure activities quietly
(e) is often "on the go" or acts as if "driven by a motor"
(f) often talks excessively

Impulsivity
(g) often blurts out answers before questions have been completed
(h) often has difficulty awaiting turn
(i) often interrupts or intrudes on others (e.g., butts into conversations)

B. Some hyperactive-impulsive or inattentive symptoms caused impairment before age 7.

C. Some impairment from the symptoms occurs in two or more settings (e.g., school and home)

D. There is clear evidence of clinically significant impairment in social, academic, or occupational functioning.

E. The symptoms do not occur exclusively during the course of a Pervasive Developmental Disorder or Psychotic Disorder or Mood Disorder.

traditional treatments for ADHD such as methylphenidate (Ritalin) do not respond or become worse.

Children with oppositional defiant disorder are difficult and may show hyperactivity and destructive behaviour but are not impulsive and do not show inattention. Many parents of these children complain that their child is "hyper". However, research has shown that hyperactivity, present only at home, is unlikely to be persistent or associated with a clinical disorder (9). Many of these children get prescribed methylphenidate with poor results. In those cases, where the diagnosis is uncertain, it is best to ask the parents and the teacher to complete Conners' Rating Scales.[a] It is easy to score and has scales for hyperactivity, impulsivity, anxiety, conduct problems, learning problems and psychosomatic symptoms.

Incidence

Approximately six percent of children suffer from ADHD. This disorder is seven times more common in boys than girls (10).

Etiology

There is strong evidence that children with this disorder are born with a gene which makes them more likely to develop ADHD (11). Thus, there is usually a history that some members of the family have also suffered from the disorder.

---

[a] Multi-Health Systems Inc., 65 Overlea Blvd., Ste. 210, Toronto, Ontario, M4H 1P1. Copyright 1989.

Course

1. Children with ADHD are prone to develop Oppositional Defiant Disorder. In one study 20% of children had both disorders (13).

2. Many ADHD children develop antisocial and violent behaviour. One study showed that 45% were convicted of at least one serious offence in adolescence (58% of lower class, 36% of middle class and 52% of upper class) (14). Remarkably, ADHD is a risk factor for antisocial behaviour for boys but not for girls. Girls with ADHD seldom develop antisocial and violent behaviour (15). Antisocial behaviour is not a necessary component of ADHD, and is avoidable through good management. Preventing the child from developing antisocial and violent behaviour and getting into trouble with the law are essential goals of treatment.

3. In one study 66% of the children with ADHD continued to have symptoms of the disorder in adulthood and 23% developed antisocial personality disorder (12). Many adults with the disorder continue to find taking stimulants such as methylphenidate (Ritalin) helpful.

Treatment

Goals of Treatment

1. To ensure that the child is seen as suffering from a disorder and not as a bad child.

2. To ensure that the child does not develop antisocial and aggressive behaviour which could involve the child with the law.

3. To ensure that the child attains academically as much as possible. Many ADHD children can obtain university degrees as adults.

Components of Treatment

1. Medication

2. Working with the family so that they understand the nature of the disorder and how it affects the behaviour of the child.

3. Working with the teachers, to ensure that limitations such as inattention imposed by the disorder are understood.

4. Working with the child to ensure that the child understands the limitations that the disorder imposes and what the child can do about it.

Studies have shown that a comprehensive approach to treatment that includes medication, behavioural techniques, special education and family therapy is more effective than any one approach. The involvement of the parents in a parent support group may provide long-term support.

1.   Medication: Stimulants

Methylphenidate (Ritalin)
        The most commonly used drug is methylphenidate (with the trade name of Ritalin) which is available in both short-acting and long-acting forms. This drug increases the attention span and makes it easier for the child to focus on the task. The child learns more and remembers what is learned. Most teachers report marked improvement in the class, both academically and behaviourally. The child also cooperates more at home, and most parents report

improvement in the child's behaviour. Common side effects are reduced appetite and difficulty going to sleep. These side effects can be controlled by reducing the dose. In most cases they disappear over a period of time. The starting dose is 5 mg in the morning. The maximum dose is 60 mg. The drug acts very soon after ingestion and the effects last three to four hours. Many clinicians do not prescribe this drug over the weekend and during the summer when schools are closed as the behaviour of the child is often more troublesome in the classroom than at home.

Dextroamphetamine (Dexedrine)

It is similar to methylphenidate in its action and its side effects except that the side effects are usually more severe. The starting dose is 2.5 mg in the morning and at noon. The maximum dose is 45 mg.

Pemoline (Cylert)

The effects are similar to those of the other stimulants. The dose is 37.5 mg once a day. The benefits may not appear until the third or fourth week of drug administration.

Other Drugs

Other drugs which are used include clonidine (Catapres), antidepressants and major tranquillizers. These drugs are generally used in cases where stimulants have not produced the desired results. However, stimulants may not work or may make the behaviour of the child worse if the child suffers from anxiety or depression (16). Sometimes an anxious child behaves in ways similar to an ADHD child.

2.   Working with the Family

Working with the family is a critical part of the treatment. It has five goals:

(a) to assure the parents that the child's behaviour is neither their fault nor the child's. Parents must understand the characteristics of the disorder and that it is genetically determined.

(b) to help parents to help the child by setting clear boundaries with consistent consequences. The more parents make the child's environment predictable the easier it is for the child to control the behaviour.

(c) to communicate to parents that it will take more patience and energy to teach proper behaviour to a child with ADHD than a child without this disorder.

(d) to help the family with marital and economic problems which will make it easier for them to find the extra patience and energy that the ADHD child demands.

(e) to encourage the parents to work with the teacher, so that there is a common understanding and a consistent approach to the child both in the classroom and at home.

3.   Working with the Teacher

As the child is more often a problem in the classroom than at home, the demand for treatment often comes from the teacher. It is essential that the teacher be part of the treatment team. Working with the teacher has the following objectives:

(a) to ensure that the teacher is aware that the child suffers from the disorder and understands its characteristics

(b) to explore with the teacher whether the child needs a special class with fewer students and extra attention.

(c) to achieve cooperation from the school administration in giving medications while the child is in school.

(d) to encourage the teacher to work cooperatively with the parents.

(e) to ensure that the teacher is aware of the educational techniques which have been found to be effective with ADHD children. These include positive and negative consequences administered by the teacher. Positive consequences include praise and tokens. Negative consequences include verbal reprimands, time-out and response cost. Response cost involves the loss of a privilege such as recess, depending upon inappropriate behaviour. Another procedure which emphasizes the working together of parents and teachers is a daily report from the teacher which the child carries home. Parents then administer positive or negative consequences agreed upon in advance, based on the child's behaviour in the school.

4.   Working with the Child

A child who is experiencing problems at school and home is usually motivated to change the situation. These children can be taught techniques of self-monitoring and self-reinforcement. They can be told that the problems they have are not entirely their fault. They can be helped to find solutions to their difficulties. For example, most children with ADHD complain that they have few friends, and they are unaware of the reasons why nobody wants to play with them. It has been shown that peer rejection can create both behaviour problems such as aggression, and academic problems including truancy (17). Children who have experienced peer rejection can be helped not to indulge in behaviours which make other children upset. Through social skills training they can learn to make friends and keep them. This can make a big difference, as many ADHD children end up with antisocial peers because other children do not want to play with them. The ability to sustain friendships with children who are doing well can improve the prognosis.

2
Oppositional Defiant Disorder (ODD)

Characteristics

1. They are non-compliant.
2. They blame others and refuse to accept blame.
3. They are often angry and resentful.

See Table 3 for a complete list of symptoms.

Differential Diagnosis

It is not easy to make the diagnosis of oppositional defiant disorder because most young children go through a developmental phase of being oppositional. This also happens during adolescence. These are normal developmental stages, where the child is trying to separate and individuate. The diagnosis depends upon three factors:

1. the persistence of symptoms, for more than six months, even after parents have made efforts to control behaviour.

2. the presence of at least 4 items from criterion "a" in DSM-IV.

3. the parents' inability to control the behaviour and their feelings of helplessness. These are important criteria as most children are brought to the notice of professionals when parents feel

Table 3 - Diagnostic Criteria for ODD*

A. A pattern of negativistic hostile and defiant behaviour lasting at least six months, during which four or more of the following are present:

1. often looses temper
2. often argues with adults
3. often actively defies or refuses to comply with adults' request or rules
4. often deliberately annoys people
5. often blames others for his or her mistakes or misbehaviour
6. is often touchy or easily annoyed by others
7. is often angry or resentful
8. is often spiteful or vindictive

Note: Consider a criterion met only if the behaviour occurs more frequently than is typically observed in individual's comparable age and developmental level.

B. The disturbance in behaviour causes clinically significant impairment in social, academic or occupational functioning.

C. The behaviours do not occur exclusively during the course of a psychotic or mood disorder.

D. Criteria are not met for conduct disorder and if the individual is age 18 years or older, criteria are not met for antisocial personality disorder.

* Based on DSM-IV (Diagnostic and Statistical Manual of Mental Disorders, 4th edition)

helpless. The child's awareness that the parents are feeling helpless increases the defiant and oppositional behaviour.

Incidence

1. It is estimated that 5.7% of children suffer from the disorder (18).

2. One third of all children, with any disorder, are diagnosed as having oppositional defiant disorder (18). It is one of the most common disorders of children in the preadolescent age group. It is more common in boys than in girls.

Etiology

In order to understand why ODD children develop oppositional and antisocial behaviours, it is important to understand why most children grow up socialized (they respect, obey and cooperate). Children are not born socialized. They learn to obey, respect and cooperate. Normally, this learning takes place in the early years of life (2-4 years). For this learning to take place the following conditions have to exist:

1. A close and confiding relationship with at least one adult, who is usually there for the child. Because of this relationship a child tries to do everything to please the caring adult. In the process the child learns the values and pro-social behaviour as modelled by the caring adult.

2. Children are clearly told which behaviours are acceptable and which are not. The acceptable behaviours are consistently approved and rewarded, while the unacceptable behaviours are disapproved. The continuation of unacceptable behav-

iours leads to the loss of a privilege, such as being allowed to watch television.

Most children by the age of 4-6, have learned to comply, to respect, and to cooperate. However, some children do not become socialized and develop the disorder for some of the following reasons:

1. There is no consistent adult caring for the child. Therefore the child is unable to develop a close relationship with an adult. This happens when care givers continue to change due to divorce, separation, removal of the child from parents because of abuse, etc.

2. The child gets different messages from adults. This happens when the parents disagree as to what is right, and how to punish or reward the behaviour.

3. The parent is unable to set clear boundaries and consistently reward good behaviour and consequence bad behaviour.

4. The child requires extra patience and energy because of difficult temperament or ADHD. These children are likely to develop ODD if parents are unable to give them extra attention and the controls that they need.

5. The parent is unable to meet the normal demands of a child, due to depression, anxiety, or other psychological or medical disorders.

Course

The antisocial and aggressive behaviour of oppositional defiant disordered children becomes more serious with age. As a child grows in size, and strength, aggressive behaviour has more serious consequences. As they grow older, many of these children develop behaviours which are symptoms of conduct disorder. These behaviours may include hitting, stealing and destruction of property. Therefore, many oppositional defiant disordered children grow up to become conduct disordered youth.

Treatment

The treatment of this disorder should be taken seriously and start as soon as the child is brought to the notice of professionals. Unlike other problems that children grow out of, such as shyness, oppositional defiant disorder has the possibility of becoming worse without proper interventions. Research has shown that non-compliance is the beginning of more serious antisocial behaviours later in life (19). The progress is also better when treatment starts at an early age rather than later in life. Parents, family physicians, paediatricians and teachers must be encouraged to refer children to child psychiatrists and children's mental health clinics when they notice defiant and aggressive behaviour. *Parents must be made aware that aggressive behaviour in a child is a serious symptom.* Parents should be encouraged to ask for help, if their own efforts to control the behaviour have been unsuccessful and especially if they feel helpless in the situation.

Treatment Planning

Before the treatment plan is developed it is important to take a careful history and carry out a careful assessment with the following objectives in mind:

1. to determine whether the child was a difficult baby with a difficult temperament (crying a lot, hard to soothe, difficult to feed, not sleeping well).

2. to determine whether the child is suffering from ADHD

3. to determine if the child has had the opportunity to develop a close relationship with a parent without any disruptions

4. to determine if the parents and the family situation had allowed for the child to receive clear messages with appropriate consequences regarding acceptable and unacceptable behaviour

The above assessment is important as it will help to differentiate the child who has inborn difficulties such as difficult temperament or ADHD from those whose behaviours are environmentally determined. For those who have no clear inborn difficulties, their troublesome behaviour is more likely to be a result of lack of socialization in early childhood. In such cases, the child-parent interaction must be carefully examined in the family assessment.

The results of the assessment should be shared with the parents. If the child has ADHD or if there is a history of difficult temperament, parents should be made aware of this information. This may explain to them that difficult behaviour of the child is due to unusual demands and needs of the child, which many parents find difficult to meet. If the child has ADHD, its etiology and the treatments available, including medications, should be explained to the parents.

Successful Approaches

Family Therapy

One of the most successful approaches to treatment is family therapy. Most children with the disorder are brought to professionals by the parents. Sometimes parents themselves are concerned about the child's defiant and aggressive behaviour. Sometimes they bring the child because of the complaints about the child's behaviour from day care or the school.

The most important aspect of family therapy is teaching parents proper child management techniques. However, before this is undertaken it is important to evaluate the family situation which should include an assessment of:

1. financial and economic difficulties including housing

2. the marital relationship and whether there is a common understanding of the difficult behaviour of the child by the parents

3. the role of siblings and whether other children in the family also exhibit difficult behaviour and if they do, why this child was seen as the problem

4. the mental status of the parents to determine the presence of depression, guilt, or history of physical or sexual abuse in their childhood

5. the methods parents have used so far to control the behaviour of the child and any history of physical or sexual abuse

6. the parents' knowledge of child management techniques

If the family assessment reveals that there are serious economic, marital or emotional difficulties experienced by the parents, it is important to address these first. By the time parents decide to bring their child for help, most have experienced frustration, disappointments, guilt, and are physically and mentally exhausted. They are not ready to learn new techniques of management, which may require more physical and mental effort. Therefore, it is desirable to start family therapy by providing support, understanding and help to the parents in their difficulties, not necessarily related to the child. Once the family is comfortable in therapy, and the therapist has a good rapport with them, the teaching of child management techniques can start.

The critical goals of family therapy for ODD are:

1. to convince the parents that they can alter the behaviour of the child

2. to convince parents that a change in their behaviour will result in a change in their child's behaviour

In most cases parents are experiencing difficulties in many situations with their child. These situations include meal times, bed time, taking them out to visit friends, shopping, and time at day care or school. In most cases, parents feel helpless and hopeless. Therefore, it is important for them to experience success so that they can begin to feel that they can control their child's behaviour. It may be desirable to help them control their child's behaviour in one situation as a start. Most parents will select bed time or meal time.

Assuming that parents select to alter the child's behaviour at bed time, they should fix an age appropriate time for the child to be in bed. Once agreed upon, this time should be non-negotiable. The child must have cleaned his teeth, changed his clothes and met all other needs before this time. If the child is not in bed at the fixed time, he should know the consequences. The consequence could be that he will not watch T.V. the next evening or that he will not be allowed to go and play with friends outside.

Parents should understand that they should avoid argument, repetition, yelling and screaming at the child. They should explain to the child the expectations and the consequences and simply apply them, without loosing their temper, or getting mad. For the first few nights the child will test to find out if the consequences are real and if the parents really mean what they say. After a few trials, most children start modifying their behaviour. This change in the behaviour of the child convinces parents of two very important elements:

1. They are not helpless.

2. If they change their behaviour, the child's behaviour also changes.

The consequences for behaviour should be age appropriate. For a child of 4-6 years of age, positive consequences may include a hug and a star which could be converted into a reward which the child selects. Examples of negative consequence could include sitting in a chair, or being sent to his room for a few minutes, or missing his favourite T.V. program. It is important to remember that:

1. Consequences are aimed at altering the behaviour.

2. Consequences work best if they are applied as soon after the behaviour as possible. Negative consequences such as being sent to his room, do not need to be long, however the length of time may depend upon the cooperation of the child. For example, if the child goes to the room quietly and stays quiet, five minutes may be enough, however if there is a great deal of

shouting and throwing of things while the child is in the room
then the five minutes may start after the child is quiet.

3. Consequences work only if they are applied consistently. It is
    important that all adults (parents, grandparents) agree upon
    and apply the same rules.

It is important for parents to teach a child to obey and comply.
This is important for his safety and for his future adjustment to day
care and school. It also allows parents to develop a closer relationship as they are not spending all their time and energy fighting,
arguing, and screaming at the child. They can play with the child
and enjoy his company. A well behaved child is liked by most
adults. It is important for the self-image of a child that the child is
approved and appreciated not only by the parents but by all the
adults encountered. It has been shown that non-compliance is the
beginning of many antisocial behaviours developed later in life (see
Figure 1) (19).

Therefore, teaching a child to comply between the ages of 2-4
lays a good foundation for the future. Most children learn to obey
without much difficulty so long as two conditions are met. First the
child must have a close relationship with the parents so that the
child will want to be liked by the parents and have their approval.
Secondly, expectations must be clear, compliance must be rewarded, and non-compliance must result in clear disapproval.

Collaboration Between Parents and Teachers

In most cases, a child does not exhibit defiant behaviour only at
home, but also at school or day care. In fact, in most cases, parents consult a professional because of complaints from the school.
Parents find it easier to tolerate defiant behaviour than a teacher
who has to take care of many children. It is important that there is

Figure 1 - Developmental Sequence of Disruptive Behaviour

The sequence outlined below should not be interpreted as a causal model; there is no evidence that one event in the sequence is the cause of another.

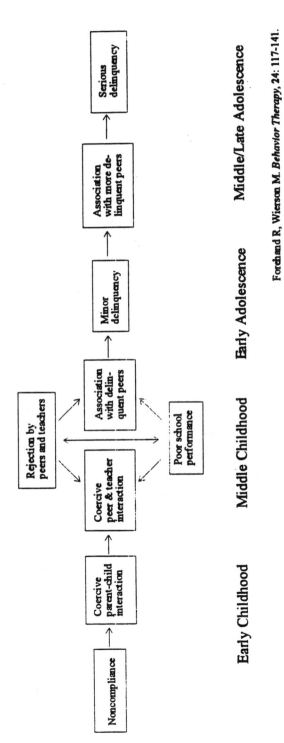

Early Childhood　　　Middle Childhood　　　Early Adolescence　　　Middle/Late Adolescence

Forehand R, Wierson M. *Behavior Therapy*, 24: 117-141.

a common understanding between the parents and the teacher regarding the reasons for the child's misbehaviour and what is to be done about it. Very often the parents need to support the efforts of the teacher. This can be achieved by ensuring that misbehaviour in the classroom is strongly disapproved by the parents, who can be informed daily through a communication book brought home by the child. Of course, the book would also indicate when the child behaved well in the classroom. There can be rewards or punishments at home depending upon the reports in the book. Professionals need to monitor the behaviour of the child in the classroom and at home and to ensure that there is collaboration between the teacher and the parent. Therefore, it is important that:

1. defiant behaviour is also monitored in the classroom

2. the teacher and parents work together

3. the teacher has the support of the parents
4. the child is aware that the parents will be informed regarding behaviour in the classroom, and there could be consequences at home for misbehaviour in the classroom.

Other Therapies

Although most children will respond to family therapy, some children will have problems which will need individual attention. As suggested earlier, some oppositional defiant disordered children will have:

1. ADHD

2. history of difficult temperament.

3. learning and reading disabilities.

These problems need individual attention. For example, ADHD children will need medication and special classrooms in addition to family therapy. It is important to remember and communicate to the parents that children with additional disorders will require:

1. more patience and energy

2. more trials before a behaviour is learned

3. more support academically then children who do not have other disorders and disabilities

3

Conduct Disorder (CD)

Characteristics

1. They threaten, and/or are physically aggressive to others.
2. They damage and/or steal the property of others.
3. They stay out late at night, against the wishes of their parents and are truant from school.

These youth violate basic rights of others, and deviate from major social norms. Behaviours which violate basic rights include all acts of threatening to hurt and actually hurting another person. It also includes the use of or damage to the property of another person. Many of these acts if committed by an adult would be considered criminal. Examples of deviating from social norms include not attending school and running away from home. (See Table 4 for a complete list of symptoms.)

Many conduct disordered youth have additional disorders and disabilities. It is estimated that 35% of conduct disordered youth also have ADHD (20). Learning disabilities, such as reading disability, are common in conduct disordered children. Therefore, comorbidity (having more than one disorder) is common among conduct disordered youth.

Table 4 - Diagnostic Criteria for Conduct Disorder*

A. A repetitive and persistent pattern of behaviour in which the basic rights of others or major age appropriate societal norms or rules are violated. As manifested by the presence of three or more of the following criteria in the past 12 months, with at least one criterion present in the past six months:

Aggression to People and Animals
1. often bullies, threatens or intimidates others
2. often initiates physical fights
3. has used a weapon that can cause serious physical harm to others (eg. a bat, brick, broken bottle, knife, gun)
4. has been physically cruel to people
5. has been physically cruel to animals
6. has stolen while confronting a victim (e.g. mugging, purse snatching, extortion, armed robbery)
7. has forced someone into sexual activity

Destruction of Property
8. has deliberately engaged in fire setting with the intention of causing serious damage
9. has deliberately destroyed others' property (other than by fire setting)

Deceitfulness or Theft
10. has broken into someone else's house, building or car
11. often lies to obtain goods or favours or to avoid obligations (i.e. cons others)
12. stolen items with non-trivial value without confronting a victim (shop lifting but without breaking and entering, forgery)

* Based on DSM-IV (Diagnostic and Statistical Manual of Mental Disorders, 4th edition)

Serious Violations of Rules
13. often stays out at night despite parental prohibitions,
    · beginning before age 13 years
14. has run away from home over night at least twice while
    living in the parental or parental surrogate home (or once
    without returning for a lengthy period)
15. is often truant from school beginning before 13 years

B. The disturbance in behaviour causes clinically significant impairment in social academic or occupational functioning.

C. If the individual is 18 years or older, criteria are not met for antisocial personality disorder.

Types and Severity of Conduct Disorder

Types

Childhood onset type: onset of at least one criterion characteristic of conduct disorder prior to age ten years

Adolescent onset type: absence of any criteria characteristic of conduct disorder prior to age ten years

Severity

Mild: few if any conduct problems in excess of those required to make the diagnosis and conduct problems cause only minor harm to others

Moderate: number of conduct problems and effect on other intermediate between mild and severe

Severe: many conduct problems in excess of those required to make the diagnosis or conduct problems cause considerable harm to others

Parents of children with conduct disorder frequently have: alcoholism and criminal behaviour; harsh, lax, or inconsistent discipline; less warmth, affection, and support; and unhappy marital relations. They tend to have large families, financial hardship, and live in poor and dangerous neighbourhoods (21).

Differential Diagnosis

It is important to remember that most children in their growing up years commit antisocial acts, such as stealing, lying or hitting on occasion. These children do not merit the diagnosis. The diagnosis is justified only when these problems are persistent, frequent and exist for more than six months.

Case histories of many conduct disordered youth show that their antisocial behaviour started in the preschool years (22). They are often identified as difficult and aggressive children in day care or grade one or two. They are either diagnosed or their behaviour is compatible with the diagnosis of ODD when they are between six to ten years of age. Therefore, many CD youth are ODD children who have continued their antisocial behaviours into the adolescent years.

It is important to differentiate between early onset and late onset types. [Early onset: presence of at least one criterion characteristic of conduct disorder prior to age 10 years. Late onset: Absence of any criteria characteristic of conduct disorder prior to age 10 years] This is important because the response to treatment and prognosis is more favourable for late onset conduct disorder than it is for early onset conduct disorder.

Incidence

Estimates of the percentage of youth suffering from the disorder vary from 5.5% to 6.9%. More boys suffer from the disorder than girls (23).

Etiology

Children develop this disorder for the following reasons:

1. Children born with handicaps such as ADHD or difficult temperament do not receive the extra support or understanding they need. In fact, a vicious circle of coercion and defiance develops between the child and the parents. This interferes with the development of a close relationship between the child and the parent. The weakness of this relationship makes it difficult for the child to learn pro-social behaviour.

2. When children who are born with no handicaps fail to learn to obey, respect and learn other pro-social behaviours it is because of the lack of an environment necessary for such learning to take place. The essential elements of such an environment are:

   (a) At least one person is there for the child, so that the child can form a close, warm and confiding relationship.

   (b) The child is exposed to a home situation, which is non violent, where people respect each other, and there is no abuse of power.

   (c) The child is provided with clear boundaries so that they learn what is acceptable and what is not. Acceptable behaviour

is consistently praised and rewarded and unacceptable behaviour is consistently disapproved and consequenced.

The above conditions for learning pro-social behaviour are similar
to what has been mentioned earlier for oppositional defiant disorder. The reasons for the development of conduct disorder are
similar to those for the development of oppositional defiant disorder. As mentioned earlier, many conduct disordered youth are
oppositional defiant disordered children who have grown up.

Recent research has shown that children who develop antisocial
behaviour in the early years of their lives have a worse prognosis
than those who develop it later (5). For example, a conduct disordered adolescent with a history of hitting other children, breaking toys and being defiant in the preschool years is likely to be
more resistant to treatment than a conduct disordered adolescent
whose first antisocial behaviour appeared at age 12. Therefore, it
is important to distinguish early onset conduct disordered youth
from late onset. The early onset youth require longer treatment
and longer follow-up as the disorder is more likely to be chronic.

Course

As mentioned earlier, aggression is the second most stable personality trait after intelligence. Aggressive behaviour, once established as a way of coping with the environment, is hard to change.
Most adult criminals were aggressive and non-compliant children.
Therefore, there is the possibility that a child with difficult temperament or ADHD could develop aggressive behaviour in the
preadolescent years and have the symptoms of ODD. The aggressive behaviour could continue in adolescence and the youth
could be diagnosed as having conduct disorder in adolescence. If
the aggressive and antisocial behaviour continues to adulthood,
the diagnosis would become antisocial personality disorder (Figure 2).

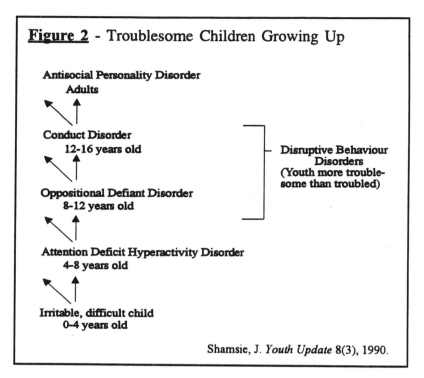

Figure 2 - Troublesome Children Growing Up

Antisocial Personality Disorder
    Adults

Conduct Disorder
    12-16 years old

Oppositional Defiant Disorder
    8-12 years old

Attention Deficit Hyperactivity Disorder
    4-8 years old

Irritable, difficult child
    0-4 years old

Disruptive Behaviour Disorders (Youth more troublesome than troubled)

Shamsie, J. *Youth Update* 8(3), 1990.

To alter this course of a difficult baby growing up into a violent adult, a number of strategies may be necessary:

1. Identify in the preschool years the children who are difficult to control and whose parents are experiencing difficulties in teaching them compliance.

2. Encourage parents to get help from mental health professionals if the child is persistently hitting others, destroying toys and property and is non-compliant.

3. Inform day care staff, parents, teachers, paediatricians, family physicians and anyone else working with the child that aggression is a serious symptom and, if not treated, can lead to violent behaviour in adult life.

4. Ensure that aggressive children are identified in early life and receive effective interventions that include working with the family and school. Given the stability of aggressive behaviour, it is not enough to identify and intervene in early childhood. It is important to continue to monitor the child and family to ensure that aggressive behaviour does not return and that the family continues to receive help when they need it.

Treatment

Critical Issues in Treatment Planning

1. Conduct disordered youth are a heterogenous group. Those, whose antisocial behaviour started early in life have a worse prognosis than those whose behaviour started later (after 10 year of age).

2. Treatment of those with early onset should include long term follow-up and a readiness to intervene whenever necessary to avoid admissions to different agencies.

3. A careful assessment should determine the various cognitive, neurological and psychiatric disorders these youth tend to have in addition to their antisocial behaviour.

4. Specific programs should be provided to deal with their cognitive, neurological and psychiatric disorders and disabilities.

5. The treatment approach should be carefully tailored to meet the needs of the youth and the family. Conduct disordered youth are heterogeneous; the reasons for their antisocial be-

haviour are varied. Therefore, it is unlikely that any one approach will be equally successful in all cases. Some youth may benefit from a systemic approach. Others may need a greater component of a behavioural approach. Some may benefit from individual work. Others may benefit from family therapy. A careful assessment, and choosing an appropriate combination of appropriate and proven treatments is essential.

6. It is best to intervene when the youth and the family are facing a crisis such as the youth being suspended from school or apprehended by the police. At the time of crisis, both the youth and the family may be more motivated to get involved with mental health professionals. They are looking for help and are willing to understand how and why the youth is in trouble.

Five Successful Approaches

1. Family Therapy

There is increasing evidence that working with the family and getting them involved has a beneficial effect on the behaviour of the youth (25). The reason may be that despite the difficulties and antagonism that exist between conduct disordered youth and their families, most youth still want approval and acceptance from their families. This attachment provides the motivation for the youth and the family to change their behaviours. However, it is not easy to get a family involved. Often they have become frustrated, disappointed, and exhausted working with the youth and professionals over the years. Getting them involved requires working with them at their convenience; visiting them at their home at a time that is suitable to them. It also involves, providing them with a reason why and how their involvement will pay off now when it has not worked in the past. Most of the time, an understanding can be worked out whereby, if the youth meets certain reasonable and limited goals in behaviour, the family will show its approval in a prescribed and agreed upon way. When setting goals for the youth, the family need to recognize the difficulties and disabilities that confront the youth. The goals set for the youth may be related to academics, jobs and compliance. The family should be prepared that the youth may not succeed each time, but a failure should not merit rejecting or giving up but waiting for the youth to succeed before showing approval. It may be desirable to set only one goal in a single area at a time. The important objective is to provide success, so that the youth and the family, both feel hopeful again.

There are many studies showing the effectiveness of family therapy (25,26,27). Several approaches have been suggested, one commonly mentioned is functional family therapy where the principles of system theory, behavioural approach, and cognitive behaviour therapy, are used. The goal of the treatment is to alter the communication patterns in the family (21). Most of the approaches share the following two principles:

1. If the family alters its behaviour towards the youth, the youth will also change.

2. Positive responses from the family provide stong incentives for the youth to change his behaviour.

2. Cognitive Behaviour Therapy

Most conduct disordered youth do not examine their behaviours, which have alienated them from the family and have gotten them into trouble with the law. When they do examine them they are often unable to see the reasons for their getting into trouble. Their thinking and logic have major faults:

1. They misinterpret the environment. They continually ascribe negative motives and intentions to others. Thus they see environment as more hostile than it is in reality. For example, A youth in a crowded room may get bumped or have his foot stepped on. Most youth would believe such an event to be accidental but a conduct disordered youth would likely believe that he was the victim of an aggressive act and react accordingly.

2. They are unable to see alternatives to the one behaviour they adopted in any given situation. For example, in a situation where a CD youth has assaulted a peer, he generally claims he had no alternative, as the peer would have hit him anyway. CD youth do not see that they could have walked away, tried to talk to the peer, or tried not to seriously hurt the peer. They have similar thinking in relation to their family. They see no alternative ways of handling their family, the teacher, or the boss.

3. They have not learned to monitor their feelings, therefore they act out their feelings before they are aware of them.

Most of the treatment based on cognitive therapy aims to teach the conduct disordered youth:

1. that they can interpret the environment more accurately rather than always believing it is hostile.

2. that there are always alternatives to the behaviour they choose. Most of the alternatives may have more desirable consequences than the one they choose.

3. that they can monitor their feelings, such as anger, and they can have strategies as to how they will behave when they experience negative feelings. This will give them more control over

their feelings and more control over consequences affecting them.

Many techniques are used to make conduct disordered youth aware of the errors in their thinking and behaviour. These include Think Aloud (28), anger replacement training (29), role playing, and group work. Some of the youth can benefit from group work. Others have to be worked with individually.

It has to be noted that in spite of many studies related to cognitive behaviour therapy, the research evidence is still lacking that its application changes the treatment outcome.

3. Parent Management Training

This is one of the most researched and carefully evaluated treatment approaches for conduct disordered children. The treatment is primarily focused on parents. It teaches parents specific procedures to use with their children in the home to promote prosocial behaviour and to decrease deviant behaviour. One of the advantages of this approach is that it not only helps the referred child but also the siblings who are generally at risk. This approach has been mainly used with preadolescent children as it has been found to be more effective with preadolescent children than with adolescents (21).

4. Multisystemic Therapy

This approach focuses on the many systems which may affect the child (i.e., school, peers, neighborhood) but the primary focus is on the family. It uses a variety of techniques such as joining, reframing, and enactments. The main goal of this approach is to build cohesion and emotional warmth among family members. Multisystemic therapy uses other approaches such as problem solving, skills training, parent management training, and marital therapy (if and when needed). This therapy is effective with delinquent youth in reducing the rate of recidivism (21).

5. Job Placement and Teaching Pro-Employment Behaviour

Studies have shown that the youth who have experienced failure in school, are more likely to be interested in having a job than returning to academic activities (30, 31). Having a job, with a pay cheque at the end of the week, is a strong incentive for not returning to antisocial activities. The essentials for developing such a program include:

1. teaching pro-employment behaviours such as grooming and social skills

2. having a special arrangement with the employer who is aware of the client's difficulties

3. having a close follow-up of the youth and the employer so that problems are dealt with without delay.

Treatments Unlikely to Work

(1) Treatments which do not impact on a variety of systems (i.e., family, school, peers) which affect a child's life are unlikely to result in significant improvement as the delinquency is caused by many factors.

(2) Treatments where youths are dealt with in group situations (i.e., hospitals, group homes, correctional facilities) may result in increased delinquency as: (a) these treatment situations may actually provide an opportunity for children to learn more delinquent behaviours from their peers; and (b) by removing these children from family, school, neighborhood, and community contexts they are deprived of the normative

developmental experiences which help them to adapt to those contexts (21).

Response to treatment is poor if:
• onset of behaviour is early (before age 10)
• child has more than one disorder
• child is from a poor family
• child is from a single parent family
• parents have a history of antisocial behaviour in their childhood

Medication

As conduct disordered youth may also have additional disorders, medications appropriate for those disorders will be needed. These may include antidepressants for depression, carbamazepine (Tegretol) for temperal lobe epilepsy, lithium carbonate for manic episodes and Ritalin for ADHD.

For conduct disorder itself, medications have a limited role to play. In a recent study lithium carbonate was shown to be effective in controlling aggression in conduct disordered youth (32). A trial of this drug may be justifiable for extremely aggressive youth.

Conduct disordered youth who have trouble controlling anger may be persuaded to use major tranquillizers when they feel they need help controlling their anger. An order for such tranquilizers can be written for them, which is given to them at their request.

Maintaining Improvement

Many studies have indicated that many youth show improvement while in treatment, however, once the treatment is stopped and the youth is back in the community, antisocial behaviour returns.. Therefore studies determining the effectiveness of treatment without follow up report much higher success rates than studies with long-term follow-up (24).

Conduct disordered youth, whose antisocial behaviour started in early childhood and who respond poorly to treatment, usually receive treatment from many different agencies during many years of their development (22). The involvement of many agencies results in the child and the family having to put up with repeated assessments as each agency wants its own professionals to carry out tests. Repeated assessment by different agencies is not only cumbersome to the family it is also expensive and uneconomical. Each agency may have a different emphasis or approach, with little learning from the past, thus providing no continuity of care. If the treatment was continued with the same agency over the years, it would not only avoid repeated assessments, but allow greater understanding of the child and the family, and promote learning as to what works and what does not work with a child and family.

Continuity of care does not imply that the youth needs to be in active treatment for many years. Given the chronicity of the disorder, these youth tend to return to their antisocial behaviour after a lapse of time. It is important that the agency continue to keep in touch with the youth and the family after the active phase of treatment is over. This serves two purposes. First, due to ongoing contact, it may be possible to help the youth avoid getting into serious trouble. Secondly, if the youth does get into trouble the agency can move back to active treatment from follow-up, thus avoiding involvement with other agencies.

Summary and Conclusions

1. It is important to remember that ADHD, ODD and CD form the largest group of children brought to mental health centres.

2. Although these disorders are described as separate entities, it is possible that the same child may have all three disorders at different stages of development from childhood to adolescence (see Figure 2).

3. There is a great deal of overlap among these disorders. Many children suffer from more than one disorder.

4. Aggressive behaviour in a child must be seen as a serious symptom, deserving investigation and, if necessary, intervention.

5. If not treated successfully, these children carry their antisocial behaviour into adulthood. Many violent adult criminals were aggressive children.

6. It is easier and the success rate is higher if the aggressive behaviour is treated in early childhood rather than in adolescence. It fact, the earlier the intervention, the higher the success rate.

7. Youth with multiple disorders, early onset, and those from the least supportive families are the toughest challenge in treatment.

8. Aggression is the most stable personality trait after intelligence. Therefore, there is a high rate of recidivism following the treat-

ment of antisocial youth. It is important that there is follow-up and interventions when necessary. The treatment follow-up and interventions should be made by the same agency in order to provide continuity of care.

9. Children with antisocial behaviours generate community expenses throughout their lives as they involve many systems including mental health, justice, special education, and social services. In fact, disruptive behaviour disorders are the most costly mental health problems.

APPENDIX:
Quick Reference
Guide

APPENDIX: QUICK REFERENCE GUIDE

	ADHD	ODD	CD
CHARACTERISTICS	1. cannot concentrate 2. impulsive 3. hyperactive	1. non-compliant 2. blame others 3. angry & resentful	1. aggression 2. property crimes 3. truancy
APPROX. AGE	4-8	8-12	12-16
INCIDENCE	approx. 6% children boys:girls = 7:1	approx. 5.7%	approx. 5.5%
ETIOLOGY	genetic disorder	1. no close relationship with an adult 2. ADHD or difficult temperament 3. poor child management techniques	1. no close relationship with an adult 2. ADHD or difficult temperament 3. poor child management techniques

	ADHD	ODD	CD
COURSE	symptoms usually continue into adulthood	many develop conduct disorder	many develop antisocial personality disorder
TREATMENT	1. medication 2. work with family 3. work with child 4. work with teachers	1. family therapy 2. parents and teachers working together	1. family therapy 2. cognitive behaviour therapy 3. job placement and employment skills

References

1. Susman EJ. Psychobiological, contextual, and psychobiolgical interactions: A developmental perspective on conduct disorder. *Development and Psychopathology* 1993; 5(1/2): 181-190.

2. Richters, JE, Cicchetti, D. Mark Twain meets DSM-III-R: Conduct disorder, development, and the concept of harmful dysfunction. *Development and Psychopathology* 1993; 5(1/2): 5-30.

3. Maziade M, Caron C, Cote R, Mérette C, Bernier H, Laplante B, Boutin P, Thivierge J. Psychiatric status of adolescents who had extreme temperaments at age seven. *American Journal of Psychiatry* 1990; 147(11): 1531-1536.

4. Shamsie SJ. Anti-social adolescents: our treatments do not work - where do we go from here? *Canadian Journal of Psychiatry* 1981; 26(August): 357-364.

5. Robins LN, Tipp J, Przybeck T. Anti-social personality. In: Robins LN, Regier DA, eds. *Psychiatric Disorders in America*. Toronto: Collier MacMillan Canada, 1991: 258-290.

6. Olweus D. Stability of aggressive reaction patterns in males: a review. *Psychological Bulletin* 1979; 86(4): 852-875.

7. Robins LN. Conduct disorder. *Journal of Child Psychology and Psychiatry* 1991; 32 (1): 193-212.

8. Loeber R. Antisocial behaviour: more enduring than change-able? *Journal of the American Academy of Child and Adolescent Psychiatry* 1991; 30(3): 393-397.

9. McArdle P, O'Brien G, Kolvin I. Hyperactivity: prevalence and relationship with conduct disorder. *Journal of Child Psychology and Psychiatry* 1995; 36(2): 279-303.

10. Garfinkel BD, Wender PH. Attention deficit hyperactivity disorder. In: Kaplan HI, Sadock BJ, eds. *Comprehensive Textbook of Psychiatry*, Fifth Edition. Baltimore: Williams And Wilkins, 1989: 1828-1842.

11. Hauser P, Zametin AJ, Martinez P, Vitiello B, Metochik J, Mixson J, Weintraub BD. Attention deficit hyperactivity disorder in people with generalized resistance to thyroid hormone. *The New England Journal of Medicine* 1993; 328 (14): 997-1011.

12. Weiss G, Hechtman L, Milroy T, Perlman T. Psychiatric status of hyperactives as adults: a controlled perspective 15-year follow-up of 63 hyperactive children. *Journal of the American Academy of Child Psychiatry* 1985; 24: 211-220.

13. Biederman J, Newcorn J, Sprich S. Comorbidity of attention deficit hyperactivity disorder with conduct, depressive, anxiety, and other disorders. *American Journal of Psychiatry* 1991; 148: 564-577.

14. Satterfield JH, Hoppe CM, Schell AM. A prspective study of delinquency in 110 adolescent boys with attention deficit disorder and 88 normal adolescent boys. *American Journal of Psychiatry* 1982; 139(6):795-798.

15. Herrero ME, Hechtman L, Weiss G. Antisocial disorders in hyperactive subjects from childhood to adulthood: predictive factors and characterization of subgroups. *American Journal of Orthopsychiatry* 1994; 64(4): 510-521.

16. DuPaul GJ, Barkley RA, McMurray MB. Response of children with ADHD to methylphenidate: interaction with internalizing symptoms. *Journal of the American Academy of Child and Adolescent Psychiatry* 1994; 33(6): 894-903.

17. DeRosier ME, Kupersmidt JB, Patterson CJ. Children's academic and behavioural adjustment as a function of the chronicity and proximity of peer rejection. *Child Development* 1994; 65(6): 1799-1813.

18. Rey JM. Oppositional defiant disorder. *American Journal of Psychiatry* 1993; 150(2):1769-1778.

19. Forehand R, Wierson M. The role of developmental factors in planning behavioural interventions for children: disruptive behaviour as an example. *Behaviour Therapy* 1993; 24: 117-141.

20. Offord DR, Bennett KJ. Conduct disorder: Long-term outcomes and intervention effectiveness. *Journal of the American Academy of Child and Adolescent Psychiatry* 1994; 33(8): 1069-1078.

21. Kazdin AE. Practioner review: Psychosocial treatments for conduct disorder in children. *Journal of Child Psychology and Psychiatry* 1997; 38(2), 161-187.

22. Shamsie J, Sykes C, Hamilton H. Continuity of care for conduct disordered youth. *Canadian Journal of Psychiatry* 1994; 39(September): 415-420.

23. Shamsie J, Hluchy C. Youth with conduct disorder: A chal-
    lenge to be met. *Canadian Journal of Psychiatry* 1991;
    36(August): 405-414.

24. Basta JM, Davidson WS. Treatment of juvenile offenders:
    study outcome since 1980. *Behavioral Science and Law*
    1988; 6(3): 355-384.

25. Henggeler SW, Rodick JD, Bordin CM, Hanson CL, Watson
    SM, Urey JR. Multisystemic treatment of juvenile offenders:
    effects on adolescent behaviour and family interaction. *De-
    velopment and Psychopathology* 1986; 22: 132-141.

26. Gordon DA, Arbuthnot J. Individual, group and family inter-
    ventions. In: Quay HC, ed. *Handbook of Juvenile Delin-
    quency.* New York: John Wiley And Sons, 1987: 290-324.

27. Alexander JF, Parson BV. Short-term behavioral intervention
    with delinquent families: impact on family processes and re-
    cidivism. *Journal of Abnormal Psychology* 1973; 81: 219-
    225.

28. Camp BW, Bash MS. *Think Aloud: Increasing Social and
    Cognitive Skills — A Problem Solving Program for Chil-
    dren.* Champaign, Il: Research Press 1981.

29. Glick B, Goldstein AP. Aggression replacement training. *Jour-
    nal of Counselling and Development* 1987; 67: 356-362.

30. Mills CM, Walter TL. Reducing juvenile delinquency: a be-
    havioural-employment intervention program. In: Stumphauzer
    JS, ed. *Progress in Behaviour Therapy With Delinquents.*
    Springfield IL: C.C. Thomas 1979: 287-301.

31. Shore MF, Massimo JL. 15 years after treatment: a follow-up study of comprehensive vocationally-oriented psycho-therapy. *American Journal of Orthopsychiatry* 1979; 49(2): 240-245.

32. Cambell H, Adams, PB, Small AM, Kafantaris V, Silva RR, Shell J, Perry R, Overall JE. Lithium in hospitalized aggressive children with conduct disorder: A double-blind and placebo-controlled study. *Journal of American Academy of Child and Adolescent Psychiatry* 1995; 34(4):445-453.